before i forget to say

sarah goldney

First published in the UK in 2022 by

Sarah Goldney

Kindle direct publishing

Copyright © Sarah Goldney 2022

All rights reserved.

No part of this publication may be reproduced,

Stored or transmitted in any form by any means, electronic,

mechanical, photocopying or otherwise, without the prior

written permission of the publisher.

The right of Sarah Goldney to be identified as Author of this

work has been asserted by her accordance with the Copyright,

Designs and Patents Act, 1988.

ISBN: 9798841631521

take this as a weight lifted from your shoulders, of words that may have been weighing you down. these are words that deserve the weightlessness of flying through the air, rather than caged in our lungs. declarations of admiration, guilt, growth and much more can be found in these pages. if you may flick through these pages and find even one that reaches into your heart and pulls at the strings,

then i will have done this right.

p.s. i have left QR codes on some of my favourites, just in case you want to listen to me reading them.

before i forget to say

a collection of all the things i have wanted to say

to people i've loved

to the world

and to you.

before i forget to say

the sun doesn't shine until it does

the raindrops don't fall until they do

you were never here until you were

now all there is

is you.

before i forget to say

i will sit and watch the rose petals fall

one by one

until it tells me if you love me or not.

then, when it's done,

i'll come and tell you how much i love you,

whether you love me,

or not.

before i forget to say

the art of eye contact

i don't think it's dead

nowadays people look down at their phones

or off into the distance

or their eyes just dart around

like they're ignoring your existence

or looking for something more interesting instead.

but when someone looks you straight in the eyes

and doesn't look away

i think they're saying much more

than when words get in the way.

before i forget to say

the loud parts of me you can't see

and the pretty parts you can't hear

because though they're a droplet of me

they are held in a bottle of fear

so i'm trying harder to be

more a river, than a dam

and i'm getting closer to be

fine with just who i am.

before i forget to say

if i am to make art, let it be wrong

let it be the page of the book that they flick past

let it be the song that they skip

let it be hung before their eyes and let them all walk past it

let it be the reason they say creativity is hard

let it be the example they point out for a failed piece of art

then let one person love it

let them fall back and look just for a second more

just because they've never seen it before

let them leave

and let mine be the one piece of art that they forget that day

but let mine be the piece of art that for a minute

made them stay.

before i forget to say

stranger once and never again

a face i once saw, or a friend of a friend

now a laugh i would know if i heard it once more

an almost importance that walked out the door.

before i forget to say

i think about tying little knots in my hair

so when you run your hands through it

you'd be stuck

hooked

bound

anything just to make you stick around.

before i forget to say

it's quite a fall you took

into my life

and straight back out again

but quite alright you seem

your bruises have healed

before i could have even counted them.

before i forget to say

intimacy without love

is like closeness without touch

it feels good in the moment

but it's not quite enough.

before i forget to say

the moonlight spills silently

through the sheer mesh of my curtains

and onto a blank wall

it creeps around the lines

and prints prison bars into my little white box

and for a while

i sit

and try

to feel trapped

i let my palms sweat

as I think of how soon i will return

to this little box of mine

and what little of life i will have lived

in that slither of time.

before i forget to say

you are the only person i know i won't forget

because no matter who else comes along

no matter what they do

at the end of the night when i let my mind free

it always runs straight back to you.

before i forget to say

you are mesmerising

i let myself melt to the ground and crawl along beside you like

a lost puppy

i feel like i'm floating

so much

that for a moment i leave my body behind.

you infatuate my mind.

before i forget to say

what if everything was different

what if you hadn't done it

what if you had

what if it's good for you

what if it's bad

what if they left

or what if they stayed

what if you could just stop being afraid

what if the unimaginable happened to come true

what if the unimaginable happened to you

what if we didn't have the ability to comprehend

what if we all went on

without knowing it would end.

before i forget to say

you are ready

and you know you're ready

because you've thought about it already.

before i forget to say

it's indescribable

the place i'm in

i can try to describe it to you

but i just wouldn't know where to begin

it feels mellow, the leaves are a little bit grey

and no matter what i do

it just feels the same every day.

before i forget to say

there's an infinity of moments you'll forget

moments that will pass

before you even realise they've happened yet

but there will be a small reel of ones you can't shake

ones that are rooted so deep

that you know

they're the moments you'll keep until you're old

they're the moments that even without realising, you hold

because like your favourite scene from a movie

that you know line for line

the beauty of a moment can't fade after time

it's been carved out

the past has been set

but that doesn't mean

you have to be finished remembering it yet.

before i forget to say

tell me your favourite song

and i'll put it on in the car as we ride along

without a care in the world

and i'll start to cry

stick my head out the window and feel my tears start to dry

because there's nobody about

you can scream

and you can shout

but this is just one of our moments in time

just another memory hung along the line

a billion different moments are going on right now

and they all matter

but they don't

somehow.

[so we can keep going on little midnight drives

   but no one will ever really know about our little lives]

before i forget to say

you locked eyes with them

for a few seconds as they walked past

only a few seconds and the seconds went fast

but your path and theirs

crossed at the exact same moment

and now they'll go on their way

to live their own life

and you have no idea what that might be

you'll probably never see them again

but you shared that one moment with them

so smile at the stranger in the street

the stranger you *almost* got to meet.

before i forget to say

you are an extraordinary perk of nature

you are a little bottle of antidote

that she drinks just to save her.

before i forget to say

swing her around

don't let her drown

in the joy that is just getting knee deep.

watch him dive in

with a string to his chin

keep his head up as he sinks into beauty sleep.

~ look after each other.

before i forget to say

i feel hunted

in the way you want me gone instead of found

all i wanted

was for you to chase me

but now you've run me down.

before i forget to say

love unconditionally

love limitlessly

love infinitely

love with every inch of your being

and keep loving for as long as you live

even if you get nothing at all in return

be the one that gave everything you could

not the one that *took everything they had.*

before i forget to say

it seems as though there are two sides to heartbreak

the heartbreaker and the heartbroken

but when you cut it open

they are nothing but the same person

one with tears behind their eyes and one with a smile that cries

to break a heart, to smash it

crush it

poach it

takes courage

and there are many different ways to approach it

but none the less there is a breaker and a broken

one that's lost hope and one that's left hoping

well at least that's what we are led to think

not that two hearts can be broken by the exact same thing

so maybe tossing the blame for pain is a selfish way out

assuming the culprit is them

and you're the one that's hurting now

maybe there's only one side to heartbreak

not the good or the bad, the right or the wrong

just that you are both in pain as you try to move on.

before i forget to say

there are flames in the field i see

and now i know you're burning it all for me

there's broken glass in your eye

from the bottles you smash each time i cry

never has anyone been so destructive, destroying

but now i think i understand

you hurt the world

because you think it needs to pay for the pain in me

how beautifully evil you can be

turns out all that anger,

was just empathy.

before i forget to say

i chipped my nails today

and it made me think of you

in the way you like everything a little less than perfect

a little bit broken

and a little less their worth

except all the more worthy

because there is all the more to adore

because someone is much more interesting

when there is some difference worth looking for.

											before i forget to say

i'm searching for me

but forgot where i hid.

before i forget to say

whisk me up and wash me away in your waves of excitement

but be careful with me please

i will follow your lead

and i will do it with ease

i have too much trust to give

and i have too much patience to forgive

so i will sit with you as your tears dry

watch,

if you cry, i'll cry

if you jump, i'll try to fly

not because i do not live a life of my own,

have hopes and fears and plans,

just that seeing the good in people is all i've ever known,

all i ever will,

and all i ever can.

so drown me in the goodness of you

and it will teach me to swim

so i can know how good you really are

when you finally let me in.

before i forget to say

today i made it home

and as i stepped back into the four square walls

that once seemed so much like a prison

the sun that leaked through the windows

and cast shadowed bars on my wall

seemed back then like i was missing out on it all

trapped and instead of flying the nest i was starting to fall

but now the walls give me space to breathe

and the sun floods out rather than in

my bed sheets are light, they don't weigh me down anymore

and the window is a place where i go to look out

and decide where i'm going to begin

there was something relieving about leaving here

it felt good to get out on my own

but there is something even more relieving about coming back

free and grown

knowing there really is no place like home.

before i forget to say

she is like honey

she is like fire

she is warm but you won't see her cry

her feet are always a little off the ground

she is quiet but you'll fall in love with the sound

of the way she clicks her tongue when she's thinking hard

enough and the way she sinks into herself

when times are getting tough

the walk she walks, well you could spot her from the moon

in a hurricane, a storm, tsunami

you can bet she'd make it through

she watches TV but only the dumb kind

and only to kill a few brain cells

because sometimes her brain gets full and when it does

oh you can tell

and in the evening when she's tired, she will curl up in a ball

like a snail, in the corner, and she'll get really small

and as she slips away for another day

she will start to melt

leaving behind all of the feeling of today that she had felt.

before i forget to say

i think that secretly i really miss you

and i say secretly because even i didn't know it until now

i know that it has been bottled up in a tiny corner in my heart

and it's only just washed up somehow

i think i ignore the fact i miss you

because i know you're not going anywhere

but then a home seems stable until it's ripped up by a storm

a heart seems warm until it's frozen to the core

there is nothing about loving you that makes us permanent

we are both just human, you see

but i want you to know that

you are the start and end of me.

i could tell you this 100x over

and it still wouldn't be enough to last

but i would rather you hear it echo around your eardrums

i'd rather you be sick of knowing

than forget to say.

so my days of throwing secrets in bottles

into the ocean of my heart,

i'm leaving in the past.

before i forget to say

an honest laugh

is contagious

and spreads quick, like disease

a proper laugh

will bring you to your knees

a two chins

closed eyes

silent kind of wheeze

a smile that isn't forced like you're pretending to say cheese

but a teeth on show

struggling to breathe

nearly brings on a tear

that's the kind of laughter you really want to hear.

before i forget to say

being completely naked

nothing but with what you started

beautifully crafted

clothes stripped and skin bare

nothing touching your back but your hair

and with that,

your mask removed

all your eyes can do is tell the truth

the words you spit out are crumpled and chewed

and the rose in your cheeks

starts to clamber up and across your nose

as your heart starts to pound as it knows you're exposed

because it wants to get out too

let all the feelings lay out on display with you

you want to be seen

and it knows you do.

so when you can wear your heart on your chest

or let it slip down to your sleeve

that's when you can be completely naked

with ease.

before i forget to say

if nothing else

let me be following you

look over your shoulder and watch

as i slip into your footprints

ten miles behind

i don't know where you're going

but i know that you're kind.

before i forget to say

my earlobe is attached

yours isn't.

i decided where i'm going

you didn't.

i knew what i wanted

you didn't have a clue

you were looking around

i was looking at you.

isn't it strange, i spot so many differences now,

than before.

but our different earlobes

is the first thing i saw.

before i forget to say

her hair falls a little too perfect

even as the door opens it doesn't disturb it

she is silent and still

and overflowing with charm

unravelling gracefully as her bag slides off her arm

she's got to be something out of a movie

there's no other way

or maybe i am just dreaming today.

and i must be

because as she gets up to move, she melts into the crowd

and what i would give

for the train to unwind

and my gum be unchewed

just to re-see

my stranger on the tube.

before i forget to say

once it's over

and you've got past the feeling of empty

so slowly, and i mean slowly

you're starting to fill up again, starting to feel again

in your head and your heart

putting back the pieces that had been ripped apart

but as you hold the parts together, trying to let them re-grow

you realise, it's not about what you feel now

it's about what you know

you are weaker now, but wiser

and i guess it was fate

that kicked you down this well and put poison on your plate

but that's how you know you're learning

because now you'd never take a bite

though the drug she used to kiss you with

you deemed quite alright

so you're filling yourself back up now

but it's a god damn long wait

because you check everything for poison

that arrives on your plate.

before i forget to say

i know you're tired of healing broken people

because it is not your job

but everyone is broken.

i think what you need to wait around for

is someone whose missing pieces

can be found in you

someone who is broken *perfectly*

so you don't feel the need to piece them back together

and that'll be it

because there is someone out there

who

even though they are broken

they are the perfect fit.

before i forget to say

pour a glass of wine down my new white t-shirt

and let it stain me red

spit out a terrible chat up line

and coax me back to bed

but whatever you do

don't get inside my head.

before i forget to say

in the moments between my tear falling from my eye and rolling

down to my chin, sitting, on fire, as we've just finished arguing

every ounce of my skin trembles with rage

usually my thoughts come in straight lines, like a piece of string

but after 12 minutes of override and word vomiting

it's more of a string full of knots that seems impossible to untie

and the thought of ripping my fingers trying to think straight again

hurts my head even more, now my brain is all fried

so as the droplet slides over my cheek, glowing red

i think about switching myself off, i think about going to bed

but then the taste of salt, as it seeps past the corner of my lip

and the knots all but simply loosen their grip

because i know saltiness isn't a flavour

nor feeling worth holding onto

and it's not worth our time

for me to try and suck an apology from you

i decide the salt is too bitter and instead taste the sweetness of "sorry"

building on my tongue

so as the tear reaches the edge of my chin, just before it drops

i wipe it away and use it to dampen my rage

and all of a sudden, the fire

it stops.

before i forget to say

all jokes aside

if the rules didn't abide

i'd want to make this serious

but i know how it ends

you're my best friend

and i'm not that delirious.

before i forget to say

he could talk for England

he could even talk for Italy or Spain

if they asked.

but what he cannot do

is speak from his heart.

before i forget to say

all you feel is the warmth of her smile

the soft kisses on your forehead

and your cheeks

and your nose

her love filled hugs are all you've ever known

now its 20 years later

you're just now realising

that she might well have needed that hug too

and her smile was only warm

because she cranked up the heat of her heart just for you

the love she poured over you like sweet honey

was drained from her like a bank robbed of money

but you understand

that although you were taking it all without knowing

you were the only thing that was keeping her going.

before i forget to say

when you strum the strings on your guitar just right

and it sounds

undeniably

beautiful

and for as long as that sound rings on

you know that right where you are

is perfect

for now

i've never found such a medicine as music

but if it makes me feel like this

then i'd be stupid not to use it.

before i forget to say

stepping out of your comfort zone

is like jumping out of a plane

you're sat

dangling your legs over the edge

driving yourself insane

grasping the sides with your fingertips

you really want to let go

you're really

really

trying

but all you have to do

is loosen your grip

and all of a sudden

you're flying.

before i forget to say

started feeling it again

don't ask me how

don't ask me when

but all i feel is it pinching my gut

squeezing my brain

and poaching my heart

all over again.

before i forget to say

no matter how close to you i get

i hold out my arm

and i still can't reach you yet

even when we hug

and our hearts are so close

they could practically knock on each other's doors

why do you still feel so far away?

~ i hope my arm has grown a little bit longer today.

before i forget to say

the biggest lie will always be

how big you make yourself seem

how close

so i will jump up and sprint all the way down to the beach

just to realise

you've tricked me

and you're always out of reach.

~to the sun

before i forget to say

looking around is like a shot of amnesia

for a second it feels like i am stood in a room

dotted with strangers

each one of them

a projection

or a fake

for a moment i forget that these are people i have known

people around which i've grown

or maybe that is the problem

maybe my growth is stunted

because i've been in too small a pot

for too long

maybe this small pot of soil

this room full of strangers

is not where i belong.

before i forget to say

there's a thunderstorm in the attic

just along the corridor

and up a flight of stairs

they say that it's a big one that could cause a lot of damage

but no one seems to care

it's so heavy up there

it's leaking through the floorboards and dripping onto my bed

it's loud

and i can hear things being thrashed around

but no one else is complaining about the sound

i have no idea how long it will last

so

i will just sit in this puddle on my bed

and wait for it to pass.

before i forget to say

i'm inside

but i'd rather be out

i'm whispering

but i'd rather shout

there's plenty of things i'd rather be doing right now

but i'd rather be no one but me

somehow.

before i forget to say

remake the world

for it is only how you view it

screw it all up

and just

redo it.

before i forget to say

for the first time in forever

there's only one thing that i want

and the worst part is

i know i can reach it

i'm just too scared

that it will slip through my fingers.

before i forget to say

count me in

if every second is going to feel like our first

if my heart will continue to feel like it could burst

if i will stop worrying if the flowers will bloom or die

if i will continue to ride this wave of a high

it feels like this is where it will begin

and it feels fun

so count me in.

before i forget to say

sometimes i find it hard to comprehend the size of us

how important we are in the grand scheme of things

in the moving's of it all

i cannot understand the importance of us in a world so big

when we are so small

how the things we do and the things we say

can make a change to it all

us and all we are seem insignificant, unimportant

and despite the masses, me and you,

well, there doesn't seem to be much at all

of great importance that we can do

and though i cannot understand how we are significant

right now

the importance of you seems something i have never struggled

to comprehend

somehow

though there's you and i and all the people on the earth

of all of them

it makes sense to me

that you're the one with all the worth.

before i forget to say

i wish i could squeeze all the memories into a jar

and shut it tight

and kiss it

knowing it's held there as long as the lid is closed

knowing they are safe, memorised and unexposed

but as much as i wish it

sometimes it feels like

you blink

and you miss it.

before i forget to say

it can feel like a race

like you are trying to keep up with time

watching friends and family draw closer to the finish line

feeling like you are falling behind

but if you think of it more as a river

letting time sweep you up as you go

keeping you in sync

letting it all flow

the passing of time

becomes less daunting than you think.

before i forget to say

to me (wherever she is a year from now)

all i hope that you have done is slow down

because i see no point in flooding you with goals

unless the outcome is to drown

i hope you have made a mistake that *i* would

one that proves that this movie is filmed in one take

and that's what makes it so good

so in 365 turns around this star

i only hope you've taken time to discover

a tiny bit more of who you are.

before i forget to say

if you never really stop

then you always keep going

if you never give up

then you're always left knowing

that there's an ember of desire

and the ember's still glowing

because if it's something you truly want

you always keep going.

before i forget to say

dear man on the moon,

i hope this doesn't reach you

only because i do not want you to realise

that there are people down here too

and with all the people here

i guess it would seem hard to get lonely

but i do.

sometimes i wish to live a simple

solitude life

like you

because i guess it is hard to feel lonely

if that's all you ever knew.

before i forget to say

to be care-free

care less

about seeming care-free

and just

be.

~ is what i'd say to little me.

before i forget to say

catch me if you can

but a photo

a film

a word

will only be a fraction

of who i am.

before i forget to say

from where you're sitting

your view is clear

from where i'm sitting

around all the heads

i can just see the corner of your ear

from where you are

you have the perfect view

but i think mine is better

because from way back here

i can see you.

before i forget to say

i don't know if i will ever know how you do it

i'm not sure if i will ever know why

but something about being around you

makes me want to cry

not because i am sad or confused or hurt

but because so much fills inside of me

that there's nowhere else for it to burst.

sometimes i think that my body is way too small

for my emotions

because there is no way that my emotions are getting too big

there's no such thing as too much love

so that can't be what this is.

i thought the way it worked was

you'd take a piece of me

and i'd take a part of you

and we'd both be a little more vulnerable

so maybe if you'd have been a thief and stolen my heart

my lungs would get a little relief

but all i feel

is a lot more full.

before i forget to say

i'm in love with this kind of love we have

the kind that is making me feel calmer

when usually i would panic

the way that there is no fighting with fire

no spitting out words we don't mean

or worse

biting down on ones that we do

i always thought that falling madly in love

would be like pulling the carpet out from under my feet

in a storm of chaotic wonder

but this is me being swept up gently

without any of the foundations i already have falling under

none of this is hectic

the thought of you has not been driving me insane

not in the way i thought love had to be

but i am so in love with how at peace you are making me feel

because it keeps getting easier to fall in love with you

and easier to fall in love with me.

before i forget to say

i know that soon it will be your time

and i don't know what i will be doing that day

but i've said goodbye before

and i'll say it again today.

just in case,

because at home i would never go to bed

without saying goodnight

and i don't want you to be lonely

when they're turning out the light.

before i forget to say

the first thing he'll remember is Uncle Jim

leaning over the cot, pulling a face as he peers in

he'll be the tiniest of them all

he'll watch as the giants stomp around until he learns to roll

and crawl his little way across the ground

soon he's not the baby anymore, he's the one

that's got to dodge the tiny hands and feet on the floor

he'll walk and he'll talk

and he will laugh and shout

until he can join in on what the giants had been chatting about

he will grow, and he will learn

and he will shoot up like a plant

until he's taller than little June, his great great aunt

and in the blink of an eye, he'll be the biggest of the giants

hardly able to remember ever being small

but at the end of it all

one thing he will remember

when he first peers in

is the newest little member of the giants

looking up at him.

before i forget to say

say yes

say yes to things you've never tried before

because what the hell is this

if not a whole world to explore.

before i forget to say

that one text you sent me

about how you appreciate me as a friend

i think that's something

i will think about until the end.

before i forget to say

you'll never see yourself the way i do

and to be honest

i'm not sure what is even going on

but in my head

you can never

have ever

done anything wrong

and maybe it is detrimental for me to see you like this,

but i refuse to pick out a flaw

because everything about you

is something i adore.

before i forget to say

he's quiet

and i can tell he's healing all the time

he's like the exact opposite

of a lemon

or a lime

he is nothing but sweet

and hands out words of gratitude

that it feels like sometimes only i can hear

or maybe

it is because i pay attention

to the quiet boy

that his gratitude is clear.

before i forget to say

you could lead masses of people

i really think you could

you don't need stern words or authority

to be simply understood

people follow you because they like who you are

people follow you because you are good.

before i forget to say

blink and you're gone

in a little sports car that hurts everybody's ears

is that how you got so wise beyond your years

you've always had this underlying sense of knowing

maybe you're just at ease

because your little sports car

already knows the way you're going.

before i forget to say

there are things i could think of saying

but i think i'd be hurting me too

it would be toxic of myself

to re-wind my mind

all the way back to you.

before i forget to say

people may say you've changed

because of what they can see

your confidence may have taken a fall

but you still laugh with that beautiful smile

and i can confidently say

i don't think you've changed

at all.

before i forget to say

i'm sorry if you thought i loved you

more than i did

my heart is just full

and it hasn't got a lid.

before i forget to say

i hope, like you, the years pass me by

and don't crush me down

i hope i wake up in 60 years stamped with lines of a smile

not a frown

you are an incredible person to follow

and i'll follow in your footsteps

as easy as today

follows tomorrow.

before i forget to say

i'm not sure we ever really existed

me and you on our own, yes

but i'm not sure that us

together

like this

did.

before i forget to say

i know when you broke me

you could see tears in my eyes

but just how many broken pieces i'd had to pick up

before you

is what i think you didn't realise.

before i forget to say

you drove me around for a while

but you never managed to drive me up the wall

and that

i think

is your biggest achievement of them all.

                    before i forget to say

i didn't even give you all of me

only just my lips

but somebody else did

and how the tables flipped.

before i forget to say

the way the trees blow in the breeze

and hold onto their leaves

gives me hope that it is not that hard to stay

but even if they make it through summer

you can't stop the seasons changing

at the end of the day.

before i forget to say

i want to tell you to eat right

and sleep right

and look after yourself

because i know how invincible you would feel

but i don't

because i know that learning and growing

are yours to discover

even though

i'm dying to see what's under your cover.

before i forget to say

parents

as you grow, you see the world through their eyes

it is all you know

they teach

you learn

the good

the bad

and in the end, they either teach you how to love

or how not to love

figuring out which lesson you have learnt is up to you

but as you grow into your own eyes

if you realise that the vision they were showing

was slightly skewed

try and find some space in your heart for forgiveness

and remember that this is their first go at life too.

before i forget to say

there is nothing fragile about you

even if you have been broken before

you only begin to lose your strength

when you refuse to pick any of the pieces

up off the floor.

before i forget to say

the sweetest thing is watching you grow

and letting you tell me things

you don't know

i already know.

before i forget to say

"you are all i've ever needed and more"

i say to her

sat cross-legged on the floor

there's just one thing i have to ask

"how come you are the one person I cannot hug"

i say

with my hand pressed against the reflective glass.

before i forget to say

i cry on my birthday almost every year

mostly out of fear

that slipping through my fingers

are the days

the hours

but nothing can slow time

not even the birthday showers.

before i forget to say

there are pieces of you that are sweeter

than anyone i've met

pieces i've always wished i had

so to have met you,

i am so very glad.

before i forget to say

it does not take forensics

to look for fingerprints on the knife

or a lie detector test

to tear us apart

because i can see it now

it was me

i was the one who poached your heart.

before i forget to say

i've always been a glass half full kind of person

so if the love you had for me

could be bottled and poured into a glass

i was overjoyed to have just half a cup of love

from your heart

and in the end

i'm not sure if you left without knowing

but my glass

it was overflowing.

before i forget to say

stop and breathe

this is not you against time

there is nowhere else you need to be right now

you are doing perfectly fine.

before i forget to say

inevitably

i am human

so i make mistakes

and this was one.

~ i love and miss you

   though you're gone.

before i forget to say

don't wonder when you will be getting out

of this small hometown

but rather

what it is about this place that makes it feel

as if your feet are cemented in the ground

ask yourself

what it is that keeps your world moving

what makes you come alive

and soon enough

you won't be focused on moving out

you'll be focused on where you have arrived.

before i forget to say

he's got everything you thought you didn't want

to sell

wandering eyes

10 million chat up lines

a cheeky smile as well

this guy is

perfectly

utterly

irresistibly

wrong for you.

you'd be unbelievably

stupid

idiotic

crazy

~but I want to.

before i forget to say

silence can be quiet

a lot of the time

and you'd think it would be peaceful and still

a straight, flat line

but sometimes

the silence is strangling

it hurts to sit in

and it feels like pins pricking your brain

and it's pain

because silence isn't really silence

it's just your thoughts taking over again.

before i forget to say

you've made me picky

i never used to care this much

i've met the sweetest people in the world

and i want them to be enough

but they're never quite as good

as us.

before i forget to say

it's easy to get lost

in your head

it's easy to close your eyes in the dark

rather than turning the light on instead

it's easy to choose not to listen

to things you don't want to hear, out of fear

it's easy to give up on trying to understand

something that isn't clear

it's easy not to try

and it's normal not to know why

but what are we without a bit of fear

if we had never pushed any limits, we wouldn't be here

even if the fog makes the road unclear

you're still the one that gets to steer

so don't let go of the wheel because you're afraid to feel

take the hard option

the one that makes you scared

you might just do things you'd never even dared.

before i forget to say

the flash happens

just as the sun passes the horizon

the moment where for us it's finished falling

but for them it's just started rising

it is at its brightest just before it goes black

as if it is giving out all it can

in case it is never coming back

sometimes the colour changes

people say it's like a bright green bolt from the blue

but the sun never actually gets brighter

it's always been the same bright light

things just always seem a bit lighter

when they're followed by the night.

before i forget to say

i am this tiny spec

in this tiny village

on this tiny island

on this tiny earth

that is not so tiny at all.

i am this huge body made of millions of atoms

i am an intricate mechanism of nature

full of things we don't understand

not even a little bit

not even at all.

i am not spectacular or magnificent

i am human, and that is all.

before i forget to say

as long as it takes for me to throw away your hoodie

that's how long it will take

the thing is

it doesn't feel like it's mine to throw away

but then again

i wasn't yours to throw away

and that didn't stop you.

before i forget to say

try your hardest to leave good things behind

you can't drag good things out for too long

or hold onto good memories and try to recreate them

they were perfect in that moment

and that moment only

and tomorrow a new good memory

will become a memory that you want to stay in forever

so try not to be sad that it is over

but happy that it happened at all.

before i forget to say

you could be anyone

anywhere

doing anything

but you're someone

somewhere

listening to me

you could be nobody

or everybody

living your life

and what a life it could be.

before i forget to say

some people scream to let us know

that the pain has sunk in

others scream to let the pain out

some people's sadness cries through their words

others' cries through their silence

some people jump when they're bursting with happiness

others burst with a subtle smile

~it is only when you have learnt the language of their

emotion that you can really start reading their story.

before i forget to say

appreciate someone today

just a little bit more

give them a hug

or just a smile

do something that makes their day

just a little easier to get through

to make them feel a little brighter

and it might even do the same to you.

before i forget to say

like stepping out of line

like breaking the mould

like opening a letter that isn't yours to unfold

like doing something that you know you shouldn't do

like breaking the rules to discover something new

and that's exactly what i'm doing

by liking you.

before i forget to say

in a way

instead of figuring out who you are

you end up fighting who you were

and chasing who you want to be

and in the process

exhausting yourself eventually.

~just let yourself be

  that'll be enough for me.

before i forget to say

i hope you're never the reason someone feels small

i hope you are decent and kind

i hope you are not the type

to sit back and watch someone else fall

i hope that you're good

i hope you try your best not to make anyone cry

and if not

i hope you change

or at least

that you try.

before i forget to say

and from that day

i did not wait

i carried on with my day, and the day after that,

and the day after that

until weeks and years had passed

and i hadn't stopped to wait for you

not once.

i had stepped off the platform and never looked back

i had let myself get swept up in the chaos of life so much

that even in a spare second

i would not stop and wish you were there

i would not stop and hope you could fulfil

whatever gap was left

i would not stop and imagine another life

where there was an us.

i would not stop and wait for you anymore.

before i forget to say

you don't know this

but i wish i had your smile

it plays on my mind, and it's been doing it for a while

i haven't told you

but the way you radiate

is an aspiration of mine

and it's starting to infatuate my mind

you're kind

but to my love, you're completely blind

because i am a silent lover

and i'm sure i'm one of many in a queue

[she doesn't know they way i love her, but i do]

and if silence had a sound

i swear it would tear my heart in two

because i am full of silent love

for you.

before i forget to say

sweet wildflower

you remind me

of me

growing without being told to

out and open

away from it all

not planned to look pretty but somehow you do

always

up

up

up

towards the sun

wild and free

sweet wildflower

you remind me of who i want to be.

before i forget to say

the perks of being a wallflower -

spread your arms out under the bridge

'in this moment i swear we are infinite'

in this moment we want to live

to be feeling impossibly endless

for time to stop existing

to finally open our eyes

because for a while we've been resisting

and look down over all the people at the party

we are not that different at all from them

are we

even us wallflowers

have perks from this wall

to feel like we're flying

whilst knowing we won't fall.

before i forget to say

never mind the chaos

find me underneath the rubble

keeping out of trouble

in my own little bubble

just leave me be

and eventually

everything collapsing around me

will rebuild itself

you'll see.

before i forget to say

well there's 5 things i can see

and 4 i can hear

but i'm still overwhelmed

by the ringing in my ear

3 i can touch

2 things to smell

though it's getting hard to breathe

if you couldn't already tell

but there's nothing to taste

oh what a waste

so i'm still off the ground

still floating around

on my small boat at sea

drowning in anxiety.

						before i forget to say

we were never built to be alone

after a hard day

maybe alone is needed

maybe alone is necessary

but not forever.

before i forget to say

to make a mark is easy for some people

they just walk straight into a place

and let character flood out of them

they make a dent so clear and unquestionable.

i like art

but my character isn't the type to vandalise fresh places

i won't graffiti my mark

and if i don't force it

if i don't put pen to the wall

then i assume my mark isn't being left at all.

but then just as i am leaving this place

i see a dent in the wall, not big at all

actually, quite small

but if you look a little deeper

it's the smile i passed around on the day full of rain

that time i filled in and they told me i was a keeper

the way i'd give up my time just to be there again

so maybe i'd knocked the wall on my way out

but i accidentally left a little piece of me there without a doubt.

before i forget to say

i'd like to learn a new skill

i'd like to understand if a feeling is something you can kill

and i don't think it is

but i want to give it a try

because i just can't seem to stop thinking

and every thought, every dream

every moment i have spare

i've been thinking of him almost more than i've been blinking

and it's strange

because i always said i wanted someone to crave

someone that without realising

hits me like a ten-foot wave

and drowns me in the thought of loving them

well, this is me drowning

this is me craving

but this doesn't match the way that he's behaving

so i want to know if you can choose someone to forget

because he's the one thing i'm proud of

but it seems

i'm the one thing he's starting to regret.

before i forget to say

how empty of me

to be so full of you.

before i forget to say

so i guess that is it

life has been split

but i don't mind

because home is wherever i feel found

and if that's in two places

then it's double the ground.

before i forget to say

nothing about growing up is hard

we literally do not have to do anything

time moves on

and we get older

yet at the same time

everything about growing up

is the hardest thing we've ever done

because it turns out growing up isn't just getting older

it's not getting taller

or getting wrinkles

it's not getting back pain

or realising you can't run as fast as you used to

that's growing older

growing up is growing stronger

it's learning to say sorry

it's learning what you really need and not what you want

it's learning how to heal

everything about growing up is hard

but nothing about growing up is reversible

and that's what makes it so easy.

before i forget to say

over and over again

i learn a lesson i know i'll forget:

do it for you

don't do it for them.

i know i'll get it one day

i just don't get it yet.

before i forget to say

you look at my eyes like there's something inside.

before i forget to say

let's not argue like this is disposable

let's not drop words like bombs

just to see if we're unbreakable

because me loving you

and you loving me

does not make us permanent

this is not one that if broken, we can just build another

so let's not be reckless with our hearts

let's be gentle with each other.

before i forget to say

how was i supposed to know

that sending a soft smile drifting across the room to you

would lead to all of this

how was i supposed to know

i'd end up completely consumed by another

just from a simple kiss.

before i forget to say

it's Christmas eve

and there's nothing i wish for, want or need

but as you sit in front of the fire

and i hear your soft snore

i know i'd wish for a little bit of time

if i could give you more.

before i forget to say

i could talk to you about love

over and over again

and if all you know

is that i love you

in the end

well then i have done what i intended to do

my friend.

before i forget to say

i don't think that there is one person meant for you

i think you have the capacity for more than that

if you let people come and go

well then the ones

that *you* are meant for

they'll always come back.

before i forget to say

you are a delight

you really are a wonder

if i was to name you after something

i think i would choose the thunder

the way you can be heard before the storm of you

even has the chance to come into view

and no matter what

you're always followed by the lightning

always bringing a ray of light

i've never found you frightening

though i fear some people might

because when it comes down to it

you are a freak of nature

by which i mean i have no way to comprehend

how you are even a possibility

and though i've compared you to a raging storm

maybe i'm a freak too

because thunder has always been my tranquillity.

before i forget to say

i walk into a florist and i pick out the most obnoxious flowers

i have ever seen

and they aren't ugly

i know this, just because i do

why would flowers be in a florist

if they weren't meant to be here

to be spotted and loved by someone new

~why would you be on this earth,

if you weren't meant to be here too.

before i forget to say

i have found comfort in understanding you

in watching you make mistakes

in watching you experience new things

it lets me remember that you are human

that you know things i don't

and i've done things you haven't

and we are both the most important thing in a world that

hardly knows we exist

but i get to witness *you* exist

and grow

and learn

and it brings me peace to celebrate you quietly

to cheer you on from the side lines

even if you don't hear me call your name

and even if years down the line

you don't notice me sitting in the back row

as you softly say your vows

i'll still find comfort in knowing i came.

before i forget to say

i'm not the most observant

i don't really have a clue

there's a new lamp in our hall

and it took me two weeks to ask if it's new

but when he smiles, he's got a dimple, but only on one side

and he fluffs up his hair because it's what carries his pride

he looks at the floor when he is nervous or shy

he walks with a spring in his step when he is filling with joy

i don't see much

but i see the corners of his smile drop

when i don't call him a man

but instead call him a boy

granted, there are a lot of things that i miss

but i spotted you from way out in the distance

and i'm not missing out on this.

before i forget to say

as some people fall in love

they burst into flames

others melt into puddles

some of us start to drown

and a few of us slide unknowingly into chains

as some people fall in love, they have their eyes closed

others become weightless until their head is in the clouds

some of us get swallowed up by the ground

and a few of us trip and start to fall

and keep falling

and the lucky ones keep falling forever

but the luckiest ones

are the ones

that as they fall in love

they don't change at all.

before i forget to say

i sometimes get confused by our different timelines.

i struggle to understand why meeting my parents is something that scares you. and then i remember that this is your first time doing that ever. i remember meeting my first boyfriends' parents
and how my hands were shaking as i walked to the front door.
i remember my first proper date, how i planned my outfit for days and straightened my hair and did my makeup so that everything would be just right, only to spill food down myself
in the first 5 minutes. but the thing that scares me most
is that when i think back to who i was then,
i feel like a completely different person. i feel young, and silly, and stupid enough to have fallen in love with all my firsts just because they gave me a glimpse of what love can be. but in my timeline, right now, nothing makes more sense than to be falling hard for you.
because i've gone through my fair share of people to know
that something about you just seems to fit right. but in 5 years from now, i'm terrified that you will look back and think:
"how was i silly enough to think that i loved her?"
so what if that's it
what if i am just one of your firsts that teaches what love isn't
because you'll love the next person more.

before i forget to say

she is sweet

the kind of sweet that isn't good for you

the kind of sweet that makes your teeth rot

the kind of sweet that gives you a rush that you adore

the kind of sweet

that is so sweet

you can't stop yourself going back for more.

before i forget to say

i often wonder if it is an irreversible thing

if you can untie yourself from someone

or if it is one of those stubborn knots that won't undo

one of those knots that as you drain yourself

hopelessly ripping away at it

only gets tighter

one of those knots that eventually you give up on

and it becomes a part of the whole

one of those knots

that hangs quietly in the back of your mind

forever.

~or maybe not.

before i forget to say

this might sound stupid

but it feels like

when you hold me

you're holding all the pieces together.

so please don't let go.

before i forget to say

i know that i can be

selfish

and forgetful

and a bad friend

but i need to know why you keep coming back

is there a part of me that is worth something

that you have found

is that why you stick around?

before i forget to say

i know you

your thoughts are loud

but you don't let them out

not out of fear

or because you're afraid no one will hear

but you'd rather stay silent

like you know you could

than let your thoughts out

just to be misunderstood.

before i forget to say

why did i ignore the pounding on the walls of my chest

from the start

i got persuaded by my head

when i should have listened to my heart.

before i forget to say

it's like heartbreak

but instead, my heart has been stretched

because you had a hold on it

and as you drifted away

you pulled it with you

if only i had a heart made of stone

so it could not be torn apart

and ripped like this

because my fragile flesh is pulling at the seams

and it tugs a little harder whichever way either one of us leans

part of me is hoping you'll loosen your grip

so i can try to sew back together the parts that have ripped

and the other part of me is hoping it's like a passing tide

and you didn't even realise you'd drifted so far from my side

wherever you are

you've got part of me that i miss

so if there's something close to heartbreak

i think it might be this.

before i forget to say

i can appreciate the surface level kind

but the people that get their words

from the bottom of the seabed

that's who *i'm* trying to find.

before i forget to say

i don't want to just listen

i want to climb out of my skin

and slide into your shoes

and press my hands up to the glass

on the inside of your eyes

i want to feel everything you are saying

as though i'm running over your words

like brail with my hand

i don't want to just hear

i want to understand.

before i forget to say

go and scream at the ocean

swear at the stars

you could gaze out the window

or go chasing cars

when the sky starts leaking, let it all hit your skin

lay beneath the raindrops

dance

and spin

sing to the moon

search for fireflies

notice the warmth

as the sun starts to rise

climb to the peak

until there's snow on your nose

race down the river, follow where it flows

close your eyes

and let the breeze whisper in your ear

go where the water and your mind runs clear

there are a billion wonders on this rock to explore

you don't want to leave wishing you'd seen more.

before i forget to say

this time apart isn't going to be easy. we might feel like we are a whole universe apart. like the space between us is always expanding. but imagine when our worlds collide again. it will be unlike anything we've ever known.

before i forget to say

one day

and it better not be soon

a change in the winds

or a person

or a thing

is going to make sure that the spark inside of you is dampened

until it is out

that smile

and that laugh

and that sparkle in your eye

will get watered down

as you grow tall

so if i could wish for one thing

i'd wish that you'd never have to grow up at all.

before i forget to say

people say love should be easy. that smooth sailing means something is right. but you can't control the seas and things are going to get rocky. that is just the way things go. but one thing that sticks, is that love should make you feel good. despite the up and downs of the stormy weather, with them in your life, you should feel a lot better.

before i forget to say

i'm going to try my very hardest

to put this into perspective for you now

and even though i am usually overflowing with words

i want to choose them carefully

because i would want nothing less

than to diminish the feelings i am trying so hard

to fold into words for you

i think sometimes it is true that words are not enough

but if i *was* to say something

it would be that

i think you are becoming like the sun to me

the only one that ever really mattered

out of all the stars

i think i could give you so much of my heart

that we might almost call it ours.

before i forget to say

it's like you closed your eyes

as you watched me bleed

if you had as much heart as i thought you did

how was it so easy for you to leave.

before i forget to say

it's always going to hurt

and it's going to make you cry

but you're going to eat yourself alive

if you keep on asking why.

                              before i forget to say

let it out.

you can't hold your breath forever.

before i forget to say

you're never going to love them like you should

if you love them the same way you loved the last

you cannot expect to keep moving forward

if you love them like they're in the past.

~you must adapt to the way they need to be loved.

before i forget to say

you don't often find things where you expect them to be

that is what makes them all the more precious

when they find their way to you

unexpectedly.

before i forget to say

i like it when you smile

it makes everything feel warm for a while

i like it when you laugh really loud

and how you're not afraid to stand out in front of a crowd

i like it when you take me for a drive

it makes me feel more free

more alive

i like the way you look at me

like there's something in me

that you want to be

i like it when i glance over and you don't have a clue

it gives me just a few seconds to admire you

i like the way that you do your hair

and how you wait until the very last minute to decide what to wear

i like your spontaneity

and sense of adventure

i like how you're sweet

all the way to the centre

i like the way that you make me feel

i like you

because you seem really

real.

before i forget to say

take the stairs

to appreciate the effort it takes to get to the top.

before i forget to say

i have this one thought

where he's swimming in a bottomless lake

but he's swimming up, for all he is worth

trying hard to feel the sun on his face

thing is, he's 6 foot 2

so you'd think he'd stand out

but he sits back in a crowd

he's not one to shout

he's got a wife and little girl

family is his empire

up early to mow the lawn, but somehow, he never tires

up at 3am, baking bread with a grin

and he never complains

not about a damn thing

then at 5 he is plunged into the lake again, it's re-set

he struggles in the lake all day

and comes back soaking wet

his beautiful wife holds a towel to dry his head

and then everything's alright again

and then they go to bed.

before i forget to say

you have to remember to breathe

a fresh breath is like a fresh start

out with the old and in with the new

you have to replenish

because you cannot be expected to run on an empty tank.

before i forget to say

i am the soft smiles i hand out to strangers in the street

i am the way i hover above the trigger in an argument

but never pull

i am the silent hysterical laughter

that turns into a wheeze

i am the manners that my parents taught me

not just my body

please.

i am my burning desire to see the world

from every possible angle

i am my weight, for the pure reason it keeps me down to earth

and grounded

i am the fact that i bounce my leg and bite my lip

when i get nervous

i am the one that refuses to believe that there is any such thing

as worthless

my body might be the only thing

that you want me for.

but i am just trying to make you see

that i am so much more.

before i forget to say

i wish i could freeze a moment
stop the raindrops in mid-air and let them float whilst i soak it
all in, see i want to remember a moment forever but i really
don't know where to begin. because i will have these moments
a million times over
where i stare a little too long just to try and make it stick in my
mind, so that when i flick through my memories, that's the one
that i find. but the raindrops don't stop
they just keep on falling, and the moment has passed
without even a warning
time really flies when you're having fun, just strolling through
life, but it really slips through your fingers, when you start to
run. you'd think the more moments you have
where for a second, you're complete
you'd remember the feeling
of the world at your feet
but when you start to get this feeling, over and over
like everyone you pick, is a four-leaf clover
you realise it's more than just a moment
and the moment isn't over.

before i forget to say

it's been 5 minutes since i met you and already i can bet you

i've fixed my hair every minute

even though there's nothing wrong with it.

it's been 5 hours since i saw you and i don't know

if i adore you

or if i just can't stop wondering if i'm good enough for you.

it's been 5 days and we're out drinking

and i can't stop myself from thinking

about the way you look at me

what do you think

what do you see

it's been 3 weeks and everything you say i think about it twice

are you starting to get bored, am i being too nice

it's been way too long now and all i do is think

did you wink at that girl

or was it just a blink.

i think way too fast and it's hurting my brain

the thoughts i have of you

are starting to drive me insane.

before i forget to say

embarrassment isn't real

it's just some stupid social emotion that we have been taught

to feel

when we step out of line

become the fool

or God forbid

we break one of the unspoken rules

embarrass yourself

do something outrageous

and then laugh it off

because laughing's contagious

embarrass yourself

and keep doing it until you realise

you can embarrass yourself

and still live to see the sun rise.

before i forget to say

in the opening act i would say

"welcome to my show"

and everyone would stand, and cheer

and their faces would glow with anticipation

as they wait to see what i have to offer, what i have to give

but they would stand, and they would wait patiently

because although i know there are books i could write with

what i have to say

and queues in my mind of thoughts just waiting for the day

when i figure out how to let them free

when i've untangled my brain from this monstrosity

when the ideas inside

learn how to make escapism their specialty

then

everyone would sit in awe, weighed down by what they saw

eyes pinned open, desperate for more

but i cannot torture everyone like that just yet

so i'll realise a pinch of my brilliance

and then wait for them to forget.

before i forget to say

everyone has a story

and if you read it backwards

you'll get to when they were created

but them then

and them now

should be completely unrelated.

before i forget to say

today i will make pancakes

even though it is not pancake day

tomorrow i might cook you dinner

even though it is not valentine's day

because maybe i forgot

maybe i got the dates mixed up

or maybe i just want to show a little bit of love.

before i forget to say

and here's the thing

you might get to the end of the day

and feel like it wasn't worth it

like this one won't stand out from the rest

but you could spend your time

waiting for tomorrow

or wishing you could re-do yesterday

but waiting and wishing

are both in your head

so why not just spend time

trying to *be* in today

instead.

before i forget to say

whatever i amount to

let it be enough for you

though i know it may not be abundance or wealth

i hope you'll love me all the same.

~from me,

  to myself.

before i forget to say

haven't you figured it out yet?

when mum asked

"if she jumped off a cliff

would you follow?"

she got it all wrong

because i'd already be falling with you

and i hope the fall would go on

so i'd have the time to tell you

i love you

i love you more

and i loved you most

all along.

before i forget to say

i know i need balance

and i know i need time

but how can i push you away

when you are all that's on my mind.

before i forget to say

i am happy

that i feel crushed

as you wave

i am relieved

that i can't breathe

as i watch you go

and even though i cry

i am thankful

to have met someone

that makes it this hard

to say goodbye.

before i forget to say

you're like the sun

when you are around

you help people grow

and i think

more people see you like the sun

than you could ever know.

before i forget to say

thank you.

Printed in Great Britain
by Amazon

18893050R00202